MW01340763

We will miss you!

This is a book of letters, notes, memories, and pictures to celebrate our favorite times with you.

A TRIP DOWN

MEMORY LANE...

share a memory...

share a memory...

share a memory...

share a memory...

share a memory...

share a memory...

share a memory...

share a memory...

share a memory...

share a memory...

share a memory...

share a memory...

share a memory...

share a memory...

share a memory...

share a memory...

share a memory...

share a memory...

share a memory...

share a memory...

share a memory...

share a memory...

share a memory...

share a memory...

share a memory...

share a memory...

share a memory...

share a memory...

share a memory...

share a memory...

share a memory...

share a memory...

share a memory...

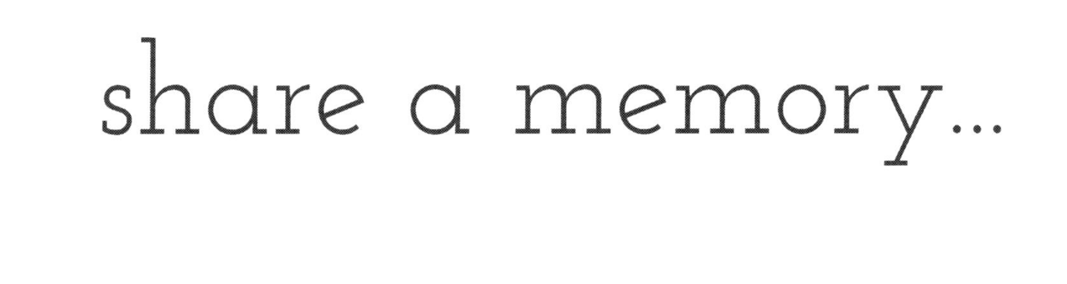
share a memory...

share a memory...

share a memory...

share a memory...

share a memory...

share a memory...

share a memory...

share a memory...

share a memory...

share a memory...

share a memory...

share a memory...

share a memory...

share a memory...

share a memory...

share a memory...

share a memory...

Made in United States
Orlando, FL
20 May 2022

18030067R00033